GLUON NOTES

WARNING

Do **not** stop now
Do **not** look up
Do **not** listen further

Do **not** speak
Do **not** ask
Do **not** question

Do **not** see
Do **not** imagine
Do **not** understand

Do **not** think
Do **not** wonder
Do **not** refuse

Do **not** turn
Do **not** worry
Do **not** change

Do **not** do this
Do **not** do that
Do **not** do nothing

GLUON NOTES

JAMIE INGLIS

© **PROHIBITED PUBLICATIONS**
MMVIII

Gluon Notes
© Jamie Inglis 2006. All rights reserved.
Second Edition 2008
ISBN 978-0-9556810-4-2

The right of Jamie Inglis to be identified as the author of this work has been asserted by him in accordance with the Copyright, Designs and Patents Act, 1998.

Contact the author: info@jamieinglis.com

Many thanks to **Alex Nisbet** for kind permission to reproduce *Between the Lines*, one of The Actor Series, on the front cover and a mirror image of *Time in Motion* on the back cover.
www.alexnisbet.com

Hubble telescope image on page 8 and satellite images on pages 21 and 39 © NASA/JPL.
All photographs and other images © Jamie Inglis 2008.

Burning the Page - from Paper to Pixel.   www.burningthepage.com
The Science Fiction Index - The top 1,000 titles. www.sci-fi-index.com
New Neologisms - new words for new times.   www.newneologisms.com
The Poetry Index - the best poets and poetry.   www.poetry-index.com
The Disorganised Society - real life is disorganised. www.disorganised.org

Printed by Lulu www.lulu.com/content/2155243

Published by
PROHIBITED PUBLICATIONS
79 Bruntsfield Place
Edinburgh
EH10 4HG
Scotland
www.prohibitedpublications.com

By the same author

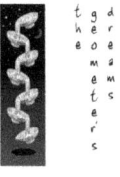 *the geometer's dreams* *(1992)*

 *fractals & mnemonics* *(1996)*

 *hold on* *(2000)*

 *gluon notes* *(2006)*

GLUON NOTES

previously

The Geometer and the Chinese Box	1
That old refrain	2
First contact, train to Edinburgh	3
Walking the Lion Route	4
Empty Cardboard Box	5
This is my art	6

some new

Gluon Note	9
Dream night	10
Warriors of Xian	11
What DH Lawrence thinks about tourists	12
The world's not like that	13
For Boa Ninh (2)	15
The next mark	16
9/11 2000	17
After the bomb	18
Walking In Soldiers Footsteps	19

Saint-Nazaire

The Greatest Raid of All	23
On the way	25
Heading for the quay	26
The Charioteers	27
Submarine pens	29
Behind Pornichet	31
Armistice morning, Saint-Nazaire 11.11.00	33
Valour	35

after September 11th

A new act of warfare	41
A Hole in the Heart of New York	42
The Three Minute War	43
A Year of Rubble	44
War Day Three	45
Six weeks in	46
Mazar-i-Sharif	47
Five years on	48

some more new

Warm Rain	51
Red September (Game Plan)	52
Mr nothing to do with me	53
Speaking as friends	54
abc	55
Saving Face	56

Scottish Haiku's

Nihilist Credo	59
Give then guns	60
Always tomorrow	61
Gene haiku	62

more New Neologisms

infogale	65
chaoshot	67
donotime	69
timepits	71

logicday	73
noleaders	75

colophon

Take it slowly	79

previously

CHINESE	**AND**		**THE**
BOX	**THE**		**GEOMETER**

prying	from	for	Looking
eyes.	all,	secrets.	at
	but	Hidden	life

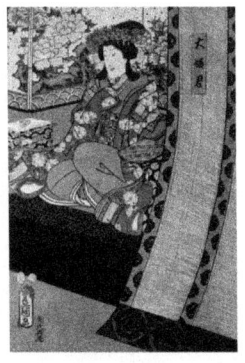

That old refrain

Heading down to the clinic again
too many E's and speed again.

Heading down to be there again
another first night, wherever, again.

Heading down to the clinic again
expecting to hear much the same.

One more time with that old refrain
something perhaps, to ease the pain.

First contact, train to Edinburgh

The fragile nectar of first contact
with hastily averted eyes
or inadvertent touch.

An exploration of potential meaning
in that moment of meeting
of two strangers, unknown till now.

But now that moment has altered
and lack of strangeness

beckons.
An intermingling of lines
perhaps love, perhaps passion
perhaps hate, perhaps danger.

Continuation as an instant decision
in a moment
of subliminal processes
hidden from interception by a conscious
Touch.

Walking the Lion Route

Walking the lion route in the pouring rain.
Down from the airborne cemetery into Oosterbeek
two field hospitals stand exposed at the crossroads.
Back to headquarters at the Hartenstein
the airborne memorial a spike in the gloom.
Down to church that will be the escape
and set out on the lion route, the low road to town.

First the railway bridge blown in our faces.
Then Nelson Mandelaburg new to the town
a quiet shelter from the torrential rain.
Halfway to the bridge, stop at the promenade.
On in the rain, a downpour to believe.
A final rest under the ramparts.
Then the stairs up to the ramp
and a moment or two standing in silence.

Here to remember
and for a moment the sun shines.

Empty Cardboard Box

I do not waste my dreams on sleep
I dream my dreams by day.

Living these dreams
I am just unable to lock away.

I do not dream of islands
but follow the flow by day.

Living these dreams
in the harsh light of play.

I do not dream of flying
nothing clouds my dreams by day.

Living this dream
of finding somewhere to stay.

This is my art

This is my art and this is me
what you get is what you see.

Don't ask me why this is me.

This is my art and this is me
what you see is what you get.

It's all of me and nothing yet.

some new

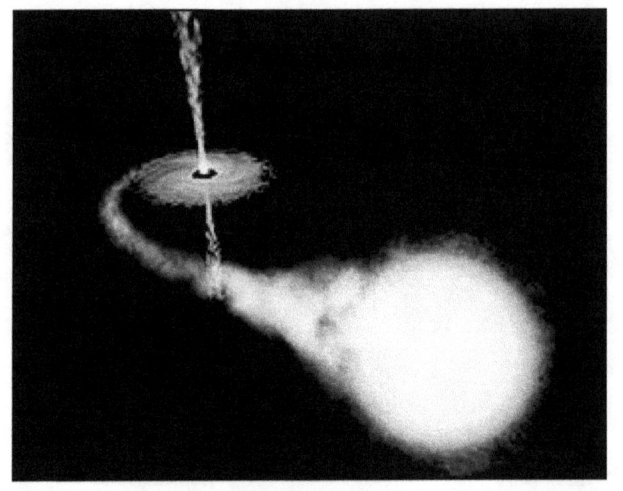

Gluon Note

Give me time
and I will take you anywhere.
Give me a second
and I will take you to a star.

Give me time
and I will make you anywhere.
Give me a lifetime
and I will make you a star.

Gluon

There are eight different types of gluon: they have no mass, travel at the speed of light and have colour and anti-colour. Their behaviour is described by the theory of quantum chromodynamics.
O*xford Paperback Encyclopaedia,* © *Oxford University Press 1998*

Dream night

Maybe tonight
is a dream night
something to remember, for tomorrow.

Maybe tonight
is a silent night
nothing to remember, if this is tomorrow.

Maybe tonight
is another night
everything remembered, it is tomorrow.

Warriors of Xian

Acres of soldiers
arrayed in square fields
standing, made from clay.

Cavalrymen and horses
eerily silent
in the red earth.

A motionless army
still for centuries
waiting the millennia away.

A tomb of terracotta,
legions of patient warriors
waiting through eternity.

Warriors of Xian
guarding forever
The Emperor's future.

What DH Lawrence thinks about Tourists

"There's nothing left to see anymore,
everything's been looked at to death."

Fortunately you don't believe that
(and are still looking).
So you've read
these few lines

and remain
only a tourist.

The world's not like that

The world's not like that.

You don't run out

of places to visit.

Everything has not

'been looked at to death.'

You just get better

at finding good places

to visit.

Or at least

I hope so.

For Boa Ninh   (2)

Wait for me here
until forever.

Wait for me here
until after forever.

Wait for me here
until forever has passed.

Wait for me here
make me be here.

The next mark

Every thought anew
a marker of mortality.
Acquired in life's footsteps,
as the history unwinds.

What treadmarks of fate
continue to wait.
Each ready to print
the next unseen mark.

9/11 2000

The days of the Nations are almost past.

A last few struggle to a bloody independence
as the Balkans, the Caucuses and Palestine
wade through their bloody births.

The US attempts to subdue the world
with Coke and MacDonald's
whilst policing the rest.

In response Islam gathers strength
and sometime not far from now
only madness will save the rest.

After the bomb

Pools of hard liquid darkness glitter
shining black reflections from furnace light.
An eerie spitting glow of retreating heat
cooling and cracking after the suns fire.
A moments inferno of neutrino streams
melting peace, melting all in this world.

Blasted, jagged, flattened, torn cityscape
plutonium powder, dusting death around.
Covering structures remnant shards
deposited surfactant of staggering roentgens.

Only rubbled remains of megatonage force
flattened fields of every city street.
Flowing tarmac stopped in mid wave
multiple sulking naked industrial skeletons.

Total silence of event aftermath
concentrated quiet of singularity event.
Utter peace from life's complete absence,
desolating epicentre sterilises microbes upwards.
Every human a powdered shadow
imprinted forever in that instant fire.

Walking In Soldiers Footsteps

Walking in soldiers footsteps.
Battling again their fights.
Long-over and forgotten footsteps.
That lead to death for another right.

Walking in soldiers footsteps.
Descending into their night.
No-one can make them alive again.
Did they die in glory, or in vain?

Walking in soldiers footsteps.
Living again through their days.
Memories, remembered now without blame,
a candlelight for the eternal flame.

Saint-Nazaire

Order of Battle

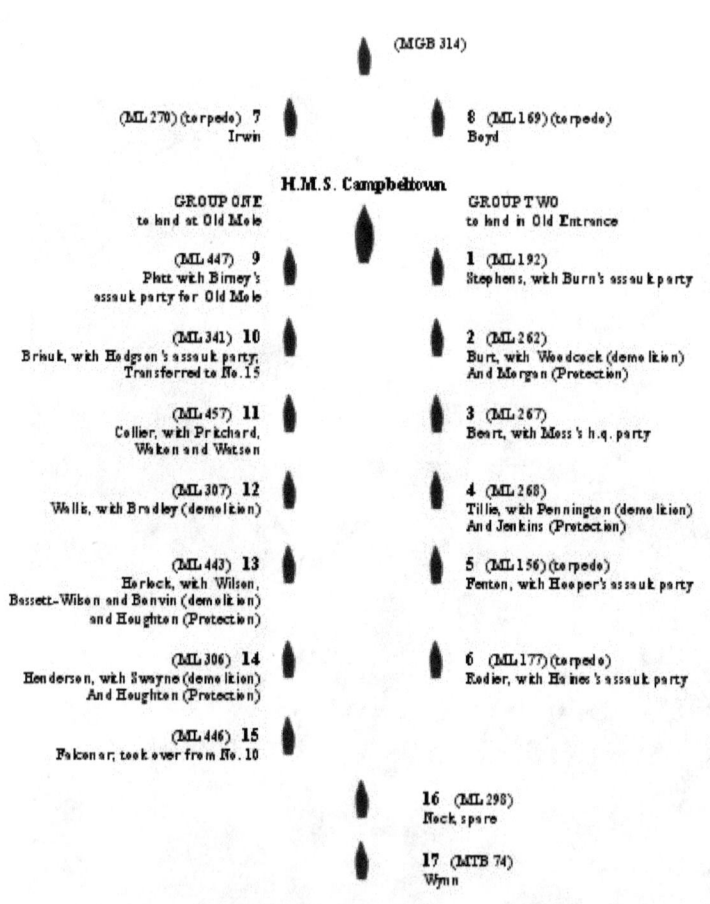

The Greatest Raid of All

TGV Atlantique.
Taking the bullet to Saint-Nazaire
to meet the men who came ashore
in The Greatest Raid of All.

Six hundred men
do battle for a little over thirty minutes.
Five are awarded the Victoria Cross
in The Greatest Raid of All.

Forgotten now
that sixty years have passed.
Remember the (m) now
in The Greatest Raid of All.

On the way

Eighteen months after the Battle of Britain
the war was at its bleakest.
So the assault on Europe began
with six hundred Commandos attacking Saint-Nazaire.

Going back to where they landed
with their friends and comrades.
Thirty minutes for them and sixty years on.
Thirty minutes for me, just time to make tea.

Heading for the quay

Heading for Saint-Nazaire harbour in small boats.
Naked under the night sky
and to the defenders waiting ashore.

I will be working late this night
as the dead and wounded appear
at my quayside site for the operation.

The Charioteers

Walking in valiant footsteps
brave men stepping out ahead.
Stepping out onto the quay
for the hour of all their lives.

Walking in valiant footsteps
brave Charioteers arriving on the battleground.
Heading off to their objectives
for the final hour of many lives.

Submarine pens

Silent and sulking
the submarine pens
sit brooding over the dock.
Solid concrete sixty years on
still impregnable
still sombre
sometime tourist attraction.
Ghosts of U-Boats long gone.
Some reminders
stay forever.

Behind Pornichet
Cimetiere Britannique

From Southampton to Saint-Nazaire
then silent suburban rows
hidden behind Pornichet.

Neat white rows of all the men
who fell that day
in The Greatest Raid of All.

No signs and little mention
of their bravery that day
hidden behind Pornichet.

Neat white rows
one marked by a cross of poppies
from a recent visitor.

A white marble circle
marks the entrance
to this little plot of (Great) Britain.

Almost forgotten now
only sixty years or so later
hidden behind Pornichet.

Armistice morning, Saint-Nazaire 11.11.00

At eleven 'o' clock
the old men wearing their medals
and the standard bearers and the band
gather with fanfare
at the monument des morts.

More medals are presented.
Brave speeches are made
to remember those who are dead.

The wreaths are laid.
The standards are lowered
and a hundred doves take to the air.

The band form up
and the old soldiers behind
march off with their memories.

One hundred yards down the quayside
the Monument des Commandos is quiet
no flags, no ceremony today.

Valour

Looking for moments.
A resonance
from the stream
that guides our hearts.

Moments of men.
The resonance of their valour
clear in our hearts.
Never, from here to depart.

On the quayside in Saint-Nazaire

after September 11th

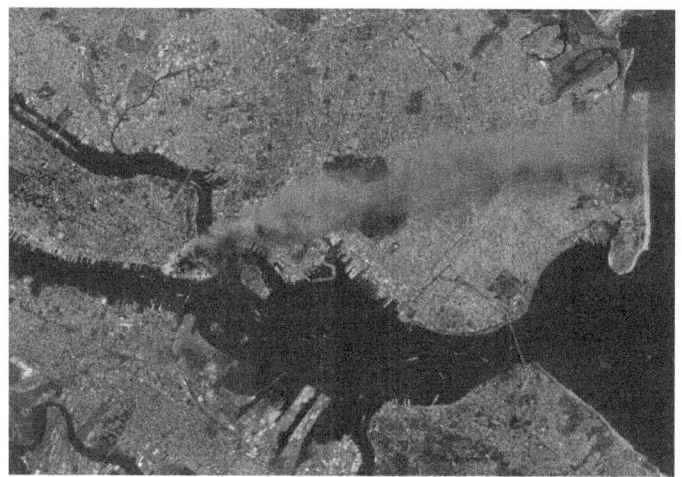

Virtual war poems.
Still reporting live
on the first 21st century war.
The Terror War.
From a frontline living room,
somewhere near you.

A new act of warfare

Terror from the air
a new act of warfare.

Terror from the air
now it could be anywhere.

Terror from the air
will now always be there.

Terror from the air
will lead us nowhere.

A Hole in the Heart of New York

Lost soul in New York.
Lost innocence in New York.

After the war started
the bodies were removed for weeks.
Then more than a month.
There was a hole in the heart of New York
with mangled bodies emerging one by one.
Into the light for the world to see.
Terror at the heart of New York.
Starting a war on terror
leading to holes in all our hearts.

The Three Minute War

The first war to start
with a three minute silence.
How long will the silences be
when this war is over?

Three minute war
delivered as infobytes
of three minutes of war
as we watch in silence.

The three minute war.
But which three minutes
will hold the truth
and seal our future as fate?

11am, 04.10.01
Three minute silence on flight to London Stanstead

A Year of Rubble

After the first hour
of the first war
of the twenty-first century.

There was a year
of rubble and bodies
from the first hour of the terror war.

After the first hour
of the first move
there were pieces all over the world.

After the first hour
we could stand no more
and the waiting started
for the end of the war.

War Day Three

War Day Three
and now years of war lie ahead.
Only the tears of Allah
and all his followers
will satisfy the US.

War Day Three
more countries at war lie ahead.
Collapsing and imploding
till Islam is revealed
will satisfy the US.

War Day Three
deaths every day in the war ahead.
Only the tears of Allah
and all his followers
will satisfy the US.

Six weeks in

Six weeks in
and the site of ground zero
continues to smoulder.

Six weeks in
the IRA give up the gun
and peace begins to come.

Six weeks in
cannabis now scores a C
and its OK to smoke, man.

Six weeks in
least news of the war today
from those making War on Terror.

Six weeks in
first pictures of Taliban soldiers
in caves in the mountains.

Six weeks in
the West begins to wonder
are we ready for the stone age with guns.

Mazar-i-Sharif

Mazar-i-Sharif.
Massacre
of men and infidels.

The first American
Johnny Span
from the CIA.

Hundreds of Taliban
ready to die
for Islam.

Mazar-i-Sharif
massacre
no-one survives.

Mazar-i-Sharif
memories
will never sleep.

Five years on

12th September 2006

Five years on
the war on terror goes on.

Five years on
the war goes on and on.

Five years on
how long will this go on?

Five years on
who knows when this will stop?

Five years on
who knows how this will end?

some more new

Warm Rain

The lights are the warm rain
of an ever beckoning fame.

The lights are the warm rain
of the pressure of photons.
Washing away everyone's pain,
highlighting even a tiny stain.
Asking always,
for a last refrain.

Red September   (Game Plan)

It is September of the year 2031.
An enormous army of soldierbots
pour outwards from China and Japan
in Operation Red September.

By September 2031 China and Japan
are producing one million soldierbots a day
in a plan to dominate the world
codename Red September.

Throughout September 2031 the soldierbots advance
conquering all the world before them.
Only you, stand in the way
of Red September.

Mr nothing to do with me

Mr nothing to do with me
he's so sad to see.

He can't help but lie
its so easy to see.

Mr nothing to do with me
he's a slob of the first degree.

What could he wish to be
mr nothing to do with me.

Rich, famous and on tv
he would (be the first to) no doubt agree.

Dream on, mr nothing to do with me

Speaking as friends

Speak to me as a friend
and treat me as someone you have just met.

We should have no secrets
and your body should tell me no lies.

Tell me only your truest thoughts
that only a stranger should ever hear.

abc

abc
I see your love for me
one face in three.

abc
Do you see what I see
when you look at me?

abc
I see your face in me
setting us free.

SAVING FACE
One letter for a Chinese Compromise

Bao Chi   very sorry

Dao Chi   very sorry, partly at fault

Scottish Haiku's

Nihilist Credo

Whatever comes next
comes next.
Come whatever, next
comes next.

Whatever comes next,
next whatever.
Come whatever
next comes.

Give then guns or
    The Pacifists Credo

If they want to fight,
    give them guns.

To let them finish,
    every war in sight.

Always tomorrow

Knowing you will never grow old

what would it mean to you?

How would you hold forever in your hands

making sense of always having tomorrow.

Gene haiku

Your genes are your memories.

They are all that remember you.

more New Neologisms

INFOGALE

A googolplex of information searched every day,
a blizzard of information received every day.

A knowledge hurricane coming this way,
page upon page of information blowing us away.

www.infogale.com

CHAOSHOT

Quantum foam boiling, tearing order apart,
unforeseen event strings, appear at every turn.

Quantum foam steaming, order fails to start,
chaotic event strings, life begins to burn.

www.chaoshot.com

DONOTIME

Time and place, here and now,
structure and style, rules if you want.

Form and function, content and design,
structure and style, rules if you need.

www.donotime.com

TIMEPITS

Forever holes in the space time continuum,
frozen moments sleeping through eternity.

Forever traps in the space time continuum,
locked and awaiting the end of eternity.

www.timepits.com

LOGICDAY

Today everything will go exactly to plan,
that is the logic since time began.

Today will be nothing that is not planned,
that was the logic when today began.

www.logicday.com

NOLEADERS

If you lead, you will be followed.

If you follow, you will be led.

www.noleaders.com

colophon

Take it slowly

Take it slowly
  see the story.

Take it slowly
  see the story
unfold before you.

Take it slowly
  see the story.
    Its you.

next

experience
engines

jamie inglis

© **PROHIBITED PUBLICATIONS**

MMVIII

www.prohibitedpublications.com

www.ingramcontent.com/pod-product-compliance
Lightning Source LLC
Chambersburg PA
CBHW071731040426
42446CB00011B/2309